GW01459988

Printed in the USA

Catalan Language
Mini Vocabulary Builder:
Stress Labeled!

BY MINI LANGUAGE GUIDES

Contents

Family	Fam**í**lia
Man	**Ho**me
Woman	**Do**na
Young Man	**Jo**ve
Young Woman	**Jo**ve
Girl	**No**ia
Boy	**Noi**
Mother	**Ma**re
Father	**Pa**re
Sister	Ger**ma**na
Brother	Ger**mà**
Son	**Fill**
Daughter	**Fi**lla
Grandmother	**À**via
Grandfather	**A**vi
Granddaughter	**Né**ta
Grandson	**Nét**
Nephew	Ne**bot**
Niece	Ne**bo**da
Uncle	**On**cle
Aunt	**Ti**a
Cousin	Co**sí**/ Co**si**na
Wife	**Do**na
Husband	Ma**rit**
Parents	**Pa**res

Body Parts	**Partsdelcos**
Head	**Cap**
Leg	**Ca**ma
Nose	**Nas**
Face	**Ca**ra

Eye	**Ull**
Forehead	**Front**
Hair	Ca**bell**
Tooth	**Dent**
Lips	**Lla**vis
Ear	O**re**lla
Arm	**Braç**
Hand	**Mà**
Finger	**Dit**
Toe	**Ditdelpeu**
Back	Es**que**na
Stomach	Es**tó**mac
Ankle	Tur**mell**
Thigh	**Cui**xa
Foot	**Peu**
Shoulder	**Mus**cle
Hip	Ma**luc**
Neck	**Coll**
Knee	Ge**noll**
Waist	Cin**tu**ra
Shin	Ca**nye**lla
Chest	**Pit**

Food	Men**jar**
Salt	**Sal**
Pepper	**Pe**bre
Meat	**Carn**
Milk	**Llet**
Juice	**Suc**
Butter	Man**te**ga
Sausage	Boti**fa**rra
Beef	**Carndeva**ca

Pork	**Carndepork**
Chicken	Po**llas**tre
Fish	**Peix**
Lamb	**Xai**
Turkey	**Galldin**di
Salmon	Sal**mó**
Trout	**Trui**ta
Cod	Baca**llà**
Catfish	**Ba**gra
Fowl	O**cell**
Egg	**Ou**
Potatoes	**Creï**lles
Rice	A**rròs**
Pasta	**Pas**ta
Bread	**Pa**
Onions	**Ce**bes
Carrot	Pasta**na**ga
Cabbage	**Col**
Garlic	**All**
Cucumber	Co**gom**bre
Beet	Remo**la**txa
Tomato	To**ma**ca
Apple	**Po**ma
Orange	Ta**ron**ja
Pear	**Pe**ra
Grapes	**Raïm**
Cherries	Ci**re**res
Raspberries	**Gerds**
Banana	**Plà**tan
Strawberry	Ma**dui**xa
Chocolate	Xoco**la**ta
Candy	Cara**mel**

Sugar	**Su**cre
Pie	Pas**tís**
Cake	Pas**tís**
Pastry	Pas**ti**ssos
Tea	**Te**
Coffee	Ca**fè**
Wine	**Vi**
Beer	Cer**ve**sa
Ice cream	Ge**lat**

Around the House	**So**bre la **ca**sa
Apartment	Aparta**ment**
House	**Ca**sa
Hallway	Ves**tí**bul
Office	Ofi**ci**na
Study room	**Sa**la d'es**tu**di
Balcony	Bal**có**
Toilet	Ino**dor**
Bathroom	**Bany**
Dining Room	Menja**dor**
Kitchen	**Cui**na
Bedroom	Dormi**to**ri
Floor	**Pis**
Ceiling	**Sos**tre
Wall	Pa**ret**
Window	Fi**nes**tra
Desk	Escrip**to**ri
Chair	Ca**di**ra
Door	**Por**ta
Armchair	Bu**ta**ca
Desk lamp	**Llum** d'escrip**to**ri
Television	Televi**sor**

Telephone	**Mò**bil
Alarm clock	Desperta**dor**
Clock	Re**llo**tge
Watch	Re**llo**tge
Handbag	**Bo**ssa**demà**
Bag	**Bo**ssa
Suitcase	Ma**le**ta
Umbrella	Pa**rai**gua
Bed	**Llit**
Blanket	**Man**ta
Bed sheet	Llen**çol**
Pillow	Coi**xí**
Pillowcase	**Fun**da**de**coi**xí**
Carpet	Ca**ti**fa
Mirror	Es**pill**
Closet	Ar**ma**ri
Curtain	Cor**ti**na

Kitchen, Bathroom, Dining Room

KITCHEN	**CUI**NA
Refrigerator	Ne**ve**ra
Freezer	Congela**dor**
Faucet	Ai**xe**ta
Sink	**Pi**ca
Dishes	**Plats**
Dishwasher	Renta**plats**
Oven	**Forn**
Stove	Es**tu**fa
Burner	Crema**dor**
Trash can	Pape**re**ra
Shelves	Prestatge**ri**a

Skillet	Pa**e**lla
Pot	**O**lla
Can opener	Obri**dor**
Bottle	Bot**e**lla

BATHROOM	**BANY**
Toilet	Ino**dor**
Toilet paper	Pa**per** de **và**ter
Bathroom mat	Es**to**ra de **bany**
Hand towel	Tova**llo**la de **mans**
Soap	Sa**bó**
Soap box	**Cai**xa de sa**bó**
Bath towel	Tova**llo**la de **bany**
Hanger	**Per**xa
Sponge	Es**pon**ja
Bath tub	Ban**ye**ra

DINING ROOM	MENJA**DOR**
Glass	**Got**
Wine glass	**Got**de**vi**
Salt shaker	Sa**ler**
Pepper shaker	Pe**brer**
Cup	**Ta**ssa
Saucer	Plate**rets**
Napkin	Tova**lló**
Paper towel	Tova**llo**la de pa**per**
Fork	For**gui**lla
Knife	Gani**vet**
Table spoon	Cu**lle**ra de **tau**la
Teaspoon	Cullera**de**ta
Tablecloth	Man**tel**
Painting	**Qua**dre

Days, Months, Time of Day/Year	Dies, mesos, moment del dia/any
Winter	Hi**vern**
Spring	Prima**ve**ra
Summer	Es**tiu**
Autumn	Tar**dor**
Month	**Mes**
Monday	Di**lluns**
Tuesday	Di**marts**
Wednesday	Di**me**cres
Thursday	Di**jous**
Friday	Di**ven**dres
Saturday	Di**ssa**bte
Sunday	Diu**men**ge
Month	**Mes**
January	Ge**ner**
February	Fe**brer**
March	**Març**
April	A**bril**
May	**Maig**
June	**Juny**
July	Ju**liol**
August	A**gost**
September	Se**tem**bre
October	Oc**tu**bre
November	No**vem**bre
December	De**cem**bre
Year	**Any**
Morning	Ma**tí**
Day	**Di**a
Evening	**Ves**pre
Night	**Nit**

Clothes	Roba
Jacket	Ja**que**ta
Coat	A**bric**
Raincoat	Imperme**a**ble
Dress	Ves**tit**
Suit	Ves**tit**
Shirt	Ca**mi**sa
Skirt	**Fal**da
Blouse	**Bru**sa
Pants	Panta**lons**
Cap	**Go**rra
Gloves	**Guants**
Socks	Calce**tins**
Tie	**Llaç**
Boots	**Bo**tes
Shoes	Sa**ba**tes
T shirt	Sama**rre**ta
Belt	Cintur**ó**
Sleeve	**Mà**niga
Sweater	Su**è**ter
Underwear	**Ro**ba interi**or**
Shorts	Panta**lonscurts**
Sports shoes	Cal**çat**espor**tiu**

Numbers	Nombres
One	**U**
Two	**Dos**
Three	**Tres**
Four	**Qua**tre
Five	**Cinc**
Six	**Sis**
Seven	**Set**

8

Eight	**Vuit**
Nine	**Nou**
Ten	**Deu**
Eleven	**On**ze
Twelve	**Dot**ze
Thirteen	**Tret**ze
Fourteen	Ca**tor**ze
Fifteen	**Quin**ze
Sixteen	**Set**ze
Seventeen	**Di**sset
Eighteen	**Di**vuit
Nineteen	Di**nou**
Twenty	**Vint**
Thirty	**Tren**ta
Forty	Qua**ran**ta
Fifty	Cin**quan**ta
Sixty	Sei**xan**ta
Seventy	Se**tan**ta
Eighty	Vui**tan**ta
Ninety	No**ran**ta
One Hundred	**Cent**
One Thousand	**Mil**
One Million	Mili**ó**

Education	Educaci**ó**
Book	**Lli**bre
Newspaper	Di**a**ri
Textbook	**Lli**bre de **text**
Paper	Pa**per**
Envelope	**So**bre
Pen	Bol**í**graf
Pencil	**Lla**pis

Stamp	Se**gell**
Postcard	Tar**ge**ta Pos**tal**

In the City — En la ciu**tat**

Street	Ca**rrer**
House	**Ca**sa
Building	Edi**fi**ci
Restaurant	Restau**rant**
Café	Cafete**ri**a
Hotel	Ho**tel**
Movie Theater	Ci**ne**ma
Museum	Mu**seu**
Theater	Te**a**tre
Circus	**Circ**
Church	Es**glé**sia
University	Universi**tat**
School	Es**co**la
Store	**Ten**da
Newsstand	**Lloc** de di**a**ris
Post office	Ofi**ci**na de co**rreus**
Stadium	Es**ta**di
Market	Mer**cat**
Bridge	**Pont**
Park	**Parc**
Factory	**Fà**brica
Car	**Cot**xe
Metro	**Me**tre
Bus	**Bus**
Taxi	**Ta**xi
Motorcycle	**Mo**to
Bicycle	Bici**cle**ta
Trolley	Carre**tó**

On a Picnic — En un **píc**nic

Field	**Cam**p
Grass	**Her**ba
Sun	**Sol**
Moon	**Llu**na
Sky	**Cel**
Tree	**Ar**bre
Woods	**Bosc**
River	**Riu**
Flower	**Flor**
Bird	Par**dal**

Animals — Ani**mals**

Dog	**Gos**
Cat	**Gat**
Mouse	Rato**lí**
Donkey	**Ruc**
Chicken	Po**llas**tre
Squirrel	Esqui**rol**
Horse	Ca**vall**
Sheep	O**ve**lla
Hamster	**Hàm**ster
Elephant	Ele**fant**
Fox	Gui**neu**
Cow	**Va**ca
Pig	**Porc**
Eagle	**À**guila
Lion	Lle**ó**
Zebra	**Ze**bra
Parrot	**Llo**ro
Bear	**Ós**
Wolf	**Llop**

Monkey	**Mi**co
Tiger	**Ti**gre
Raccoon	**Ós**renta**dor**

Games and Fitness — **Jocsifit**ness

Ball	**Bo**la
Soccer	Fut**bol**
Goalkeeper	Por**ter**
Hockey	**Ho**quei
Ice rink	**Pis**ta de **gel**
Hockey puck	**Disc**d'**ho**quei
Hockey stick	**Pal** d'**ho**quei
American Football	Fut**bol**americ**à**
Basketball	**Bàs**quet
Shorts	Panta**lonscurts**
T shirt	Sama**rre**ta
Baseball	**Beis**bol
Bat	**Bat**
Glove	**Guant**
Mat	Es**to**ra
Tennis	**Te**nnis
Racquet	Ra**que**ta
Swimming	Natac**ió**
Swimming pool	Pis**ci**na
Boxing	**Bo**xa
Coach	Entrena**dor**
Athlete	At**le**ta
Score	Puntuac**ió**
Stadium	**És**ta**di**

At Home — Enca**sa**

| Painting | **Qua**dre |

Table	**Tau**la
Chair	Ca**di**ra
Bedroom	Dormi**to**ri
Kitchen	**Cui**na
Fridge	Ne**ve**ra
Stove	Es**tu**fa
Bathroom	**Bany**
Shower	**Dut**xa
Living room	Come**dor**
Study	Es**tu**di
Bed	**Llit**
Couch	So**fà**
Armchair	Bu**ta**ca
TV set	Televi**sor**
Lamp	**Làm**pada
Carpet	Ca**ti**fa
Curtains	Cor**ti**nes
Floor	**Pis**
Clock	Re**llot**ge
Fireplace	**Llar**
Closet	Ar**ma**ri
Mirror	Es**pill**

At School	A l'es**co**la
Teacher	Profes**sor**/a
Student	Estu**diant**
Principal	Direc**tor**/a
Canteen	Menja**dor** esco**lar**
Textbook	**Lli**bre de **text**
Grade book	**Lli**bre de qualifica**cions**
Exercise book	**Lli**bred'exer**ci**cis
Pen	Bo**lí**graf

Pencil	**Lla**pis
Eraser	**Go**ma d'esbo**rrar**
Classroom	**Cla**sse
Locker	Ta**qui**lla
Desk	Escri**to**ri
Register	Re**gis**tre
Blackboard	Pi**ssa**rra
Lesson	Lli**çó**
Break time	**Temps** de des**cans**
Test	**Test**
Mark	Se**nyal**
Ruler	**Re**gle
Homework	**Deu**res
School uniform	Uni**for**me esco**lar**
Timetable	Ho**ra**ri

At the Grocery Store   Al supermer**cat**

Checkout	**Cai**xa
Shopping bag	**Bo**ssa de **com**pra
Trolley	Carre**tó**
Grocery	Bo**ti**ga de que**viu**res
Meat	**Carn**
Poultry	**Aus** de co**rral**
Bread	**Pa**
Milk	**Llet**
Butter	Ma**te**ga
Cheese	For**mat**ge
Fruits	**Frui**tes
Vegetables	Ver**du**res
Beef	**Carn** de **va**ca
Eggs	**Ous**
Chocolate	Xoco**la**ta

Deli	Delica**te**ssen
Produce	Pro**duir**
Frozen foods	Ali**ments**conge**lats**
Dairy	**Lac**ti
Toothpaste	**Pas**ta den**trí**fica
Shampoo	Xam**pú**
Laundry detergent	Deter**gent** de bugader**ia**
Wine	**Vi**
Beer	Cer**ve**sa
Ice cream	Ge**lat**

At the Concert	En un con**cert**
Stage	Esce**na**ri
Musician	**Mú**sic
Conductor	Conduc**tor**
Baton	Bas**tó**
Orchestra	Or**ques**tra
Ticket	Bit**llet**
Program	Pro**gra**ma
Microphone	Mi**crò**fon
Concert-goer	Aficio**nat** al con**cert**
Curtains	Cor**ti**nes
Interval	Inter**val**
Chorus	**Cor**
Performer	Execu**tant**
Flute	**Flau**ta
Violin	Vio**lí**
Guitar	Gui**ta**rra
Drums	Tam**bors**
Trumpet	Trom**pe**ta
Cello	Violon**cel**
Clarinet	Clari**net**

Piano	Pi**a**no
Stalls	Est**a**bles
Circle	**Cer**cle

At the Restaurant / En el restau**rant**

Table	**Tau**la
Plate	**Plat**
Waiter	Cam**brer**
Glass	**Got**
Table	**Tau**la
Knife	Gani**vet**
Fork	For**qui**lla
Spoon	Cu**lle**ra
Napkin	Tova**lló**
Tablecloth	Man**tel**
Chef	**Cap**
Cook	Cui**ner**
Appetizer	Aperi**tiu**
Main course	**Plat** princi**pal**
Side dish	Entre**mès**
Tip	Pro**pi**na
Dessert	**Pos**tre
Ketchup	**Ket**chup
Soup	**So**pa
Check	Con**trol**
Drink	Be**gu**da
Cup	**Ta**ssa

Shopping / **Com**pres

Supermarket	Supermer**cat**
Grocery	Bo**ti**ga de que**viu**res
Credit card	Tar**ge**ta de **crè**dit

16

Cash	Efec**tiu**
Change	**Can**vi
Department store	**Grans**magat**zems**
Market	Mer**cat**
Pharmacy	Far**mà**cia
Hardware store	Drogue**ri**a
Customer	**Client**
Sales assistant	Assis**tent** de **ven**des
Fitting room	Prova**dor**
Bookstore	**Ten**da de **lli**bres
Giftwrap	Pa**per** de re**gal**
Discount	Des**com**pte
Price	**Preu**
Price tag	Eti**que**ta de **preu**
Display	Exposi**ció**
Shoes	Sa**ba**tes
Clothes	**Ro**ba
Watch	Re**llot**ge
Jewelry	Joie**ri**a

Traveling by Plane	Viat**jar**amba**vió**
Airport	Aero**port**
Ticket	Bit**llet**
Boarding pass	Tar**ge**tad'embarca**ment**
Timetable	Ho**ra**ri
Check-in	Re**gis**tre
Arrivals	Arri**ba**des
Departures	Sor**ti**des
Passport	Passa**port**
Plane	Avi**ó**
Baggage	Equi**pat**ge
Hand luggage	Equi**pat**ge de **mà**

First class	Pri**me**ra**cla**sse
Business class	**Cla**sseexecu**ti**va
Economy class	**Cla**sseeco**nò**mica
Gate	**Por**ta
Pilot	Pi**lot**
Cabin crew	Tripula**ció** de ca**bi**na
Steward	Administra**dor**
Stewardess	Hos**te**ssa
Captain	Capi**tá**
Window	Fi**nes**tra
Aisle	Passa**dís**
Seat	Sei**ent**
Seatbelt	Cintu**ró** de segure**tat**
Passenger	Passat**ger**
Runway	**Pis**ta
Flight	**Vol**
In flight entertainment	Entreteni**ment** a **bord**

Traveling by Train	Viat**jar**amb**tren**
Railway station	Esta**ció** de **tren**
Train station	Esta**ció** de **tren**
Ticket counter	Tau**lell** de but**lle**tes
Ticket	Bit**llet**
Platform	Plata**for**ma
Schedule	Ho**ra**ri
Carriage	Va**gó**
Porter	Por**ter**
Compartment	Comparti**ment**
Buffet car	**Cot**xe**bar**
Train driver	Conduc**tor** del **tren**
Departure board	Tar**ge**ta de sor**ti**da
First Class	Pri**me**ra**cla**sse

Second Class	Se**go**na**cla**sse
Baggage	Equi**pat**ge
Passenger	Passat**ger**
Destination	Des**tí**
Tunnel	**Tú**nel
Express train	**Tren**ex**préss**
Signal	Se**nyal**

Traveling by Bus and Car — Viat**jar**amb**bus**i**cot**xe

Driver	Conduc**tor**
Conductor	Conduc**tor**
Steering wheel	Vo**lant**
Passenger	Passat**ger**
Seatbelt	Cintu**ró** de segure**tat**
Trunk	Cami**ó**
Gas station	Gasoli**ne**ra
Engine	Mo**tor**
GPS navigator	Navega**dor** GPS
Air conditioning	**Ai**reacondicio**nat**
Tire	Pneu**mà**tic
Baggage	Equi**pat**ge
Route	**Ru**ta
Speedometer	Velo**cí**metre
Driver's license	Lli**cèn**cia del conduc**tor**
Bus station	Esta**ció** de **bus**

At the Hotel — A l'ho**tel**

Reception	Recep**ció**
Guest room	Habita**ció** de convi**dats**
Concierge	Con**ser**ge
Bell boy	Bo**tons**
Housekeeping	Ser**vei** de ne**te**ja

Room service	Ser**vei**d'habita**cions**
Lobby	Ves**tí**bul
Restaurant	Restau**rant**
Minibar	Mini**bar**
Safety deposit box	**Cai**xa de segure**tat**
Tip	Pro**pi**na
Bathrobe	Bar**nús**
Hair dryer	Seca**dor**
Bath	**Bany**
Floor	**Pis**
Elevator	Ascen**sor**
Air conditioning	**Ai**reacondicio**nat**
Bed	**Llit**
Luggage	Equi**pat**ge
Check-in	Re**gis**tre
Suite	**Suit**e
Breakfast	Esmor**zar**
Gym	Gim**nàs**
Hotel guest	**Hos**te de l'ho**tel**
Coffee maker	Cafe**te**ra

Communication	Communica**ció**
Internet	Inter**net**
Laptop	Por**tà**til
Phone	Te**lè**fon
Cell phone	**Mò**bil
Smartphone	Te**lè**fonintel·li**gent**
Tablet	Tau**le**ta
PC	Ordina**dor** perso**nal**
Printer	Impre**sso**ra
Scanner	Es**cà**ner
Fax	**Fax**

Modem	**Mò**dem
Screen	Pan**ta**lla
VCR	**Ví**deo
Keyboard	Te**clat**
Email	Cor**reu**elec**trò**nic
Sender	Remi**tent**
Recipient	Benefici**a**ri
Attachment	Acces**so**ri
Photocopier	fotocopia**do**ra
Videoconference	**Ví**deo confe**rèn**cia

At the Doctor's	En el **met**ge
Insurance	Assegu**ran**ça
Clinic	**Clí**nica
Patient	Pa**cient**
Physician	**Met**ge/Met**ge**ssa
Doctor	**Met**ge/Met**ge**ssa
Dentist	Den**tis**ta
Surgeon	Cirur**già**
Nurse	Infer**me**r/a
Optician	**Òp**tic
Infection	Infec**ció**
Prescription	Prescrip**ció**
Pill	**Pín**dola
Medicine	Medi**ci**na
Painkiller	Anal**gè**sic
Antiseptic	Anti**sèp**tic
Cold/flu	Consti**pat** / **Grip**
Bandage	Embe**nat**ge
Allergy	Al·**lèr**gia
Fracture	Frac**tu**ra
Bruise	Contu**sió**

Burn	Crema**du**ra
Syringe	Xe**rin**ga

At the Movies — Al ci**ne**ma

Ticket	Bit**llet**
Popcorn	Cris**pe**tes
Film	Pel·**lí**cula
Screen	Pan**ta**lla
Movie auditorium	**Sa**la de projec**ció**
Ticket counter	Tau**lell** de but**lle**tes
Poster	Car**tell**
Projector	Projec**tor**
Trailer	**Trai**ler
Subtitles	Sub**tí**tols
Blockbuster	Superproduc**ció**
Comedy	Co**mè**dia
Drama	**Dra**ma
Detective film	Pel·**lí**cula de detec**ti**ves
Sci-fi movie	Pel·**lí**cula de **cièn**ciaficc**ió**
Thriller	Sus**pens**
3D glasses	U**lle**res 3D
Cinema-goer	Aficio**nat** al ci**ne**ma
Usher	Ui**xer**

The Weather — El **temps**

Weather forecast	Pro**nòs**tic del **temps**
Snow	**Neu**
Frost	Ge**la**da
Snowfall	Ne**va**da
Rain	**Plut**ja
Cloud	**Nú**vol
Sun	**Sol**

Thundercloud	**Nú**vol de tem**pes**ta
Thunderstorm	Tem**pes**ta
Storm	Tem**pes**ta
Heatwave	O**na**da de ca**lor**
Hurricane	Hura**cà**
Fog	**Boi**ra
Hail	Cala**mar**sa
Wind	**Vent**
Shower	**Plut**ja
Smog	**Boi**raamb**fum**
Slush	**Fang**
Drizzle	Plu**gim**
Temperature	Tempera**tu**ra
Degrees	**Graus**
Lightning	Llam**pec**

Government	**Go**vern**
President	Presi**dent**
Vice President	Vicepresi**dent**
Parliament	Parla**ment**
Senator	Sena**dor**
Prime Minister	Pri**mer**mi**nis**tre
King	**Rei**
Queen	**Rei**na
Election	Elec**ció**
Tax	Im**post**
Representative	Representa**tiu**
Act/Law	**Ac**te/**Llei**
Cabinet	Cabi**net**
Minister	Mi**nis**tre
Speaker	Alta**veu**
Democracy	Demo**crà**cia

Monarchy	Monar**qui**a
Electorate	Electo**rat**
Voter	Vo**tant**
Political Party	Par**tit**po**lí**tic
Supporter	Parti**da**ri
Upper House	**Cam**bra**al**ta
Chamber	**Cam**bra
Congress	Con**grés**
Senate	Se**nat**
House Speaker	Presi**dent** de la **cam**bra
House	**Cam**bra

27563125R00018

Printed in Great Britain
by Amazon